OK World,
Here I Come!

OK World, Here I Come!

Inspiring Advice for the Day After Graduation

Molly Reade

WORKMAN PUBLISHING · NEW YORK

Workman
Workman Publishing
Hachette Book Group, Inc.
1290 Avenue of the Americas
New York, NY 10104
workman.com

Workman is an imprint of Workman Publishing, a division of
Hachette Book Group, Inc. The Workman name and logo are
registered trademarks of Hachette Book Group, Inc.

Design by Remy Chwae

The publisher is not responsible for websites (or their content)
that are not owned by the publisher.

The Hachette Speakers Bureau provides a wide range
of authors for speaking events. To find out more,
go to hachettespeakersbureau.com or email
HachetteSpeakers@hbgusa.com.

Workman books may be purchased in bulk for business,
educational, or promotional use. For information, please contact
your local bookseller or the Hachette Book Group Special Markets
Department at special.markets@hbgusa.com.

Library of Congress Cataloging-in-Publication Data is available.

Paperback ISBN 978-1-5235-3180-6
Ebook ISBN 978-1-5235-3181-3

First edition May 2025

Printed in China on responsibly sourced paper.

10 9 8 7 6 5 4 3 2 1

contents

ONE

Big Thoughts

*The future depends entirely on
what each of us does every day;
a movement is only people moving.*

—GLORIA STEINEM
feminist activist, speaker & writer

If you put out 150 percent, then you can always expect 100 percent back. That's what I was always told as a kid, and it's worked for me so far.

—JUSTIN TIMBERLAKE
pop star

In real life, I assure you, there is no such thing as algebra.

—FRAN LEBOWITZ
writer & humorist

A person's success
in life can usually
be measured by
the number of
uncomfortable
conversations he or she
is willing to have.

—TIM FERRISS
  self-help author & podcaster

I treated it like every day was my last day with a basketball.

—LEBRON JAMES
basketball great

Don't ever forget that
you're a citizen of this world,
and there are things you can
do to lift the human spirit,
things that are easy,
things that are free,
things that you can do
every day. Civility, respect,
kindness, character.

—AARON SORKIN
  writer & director

Life shrinks
or expands in
proportion to
one's courage.

—ANAÏS NIN
essayist & author

Defining ourselves by what we are not is the first step that leads us to knowing who we are.

—MATTHEW MCCONAUGHEY
actor & producer

Don't try so hard to fit in, and certainly don't try so hard to be different . . . just try hard to be you.

—ZENDAYA
actor

Tomorrow is not promised. Make plans anyway.

—LIN-MANUEL MIRANDA

composer, lyricist & actor

Stop being afraid of what could go wrong, and start being excited about what could go right.

—TONY ROBBINS
author & motivational speaker

If you don't like something, change it. If you can't change it, change your attitude.

—MAYA ANGELOU
author, poet & activist

The unfortunate, yet truly exciting thing about your life, is that there is no core curriculum. The entire place is an elective.

—JON STEWART
comedian, writer & political commentator

Your self-worth is determined by you. You don't have to depend on someone telling you who you are.

—BEYONCÉ

singer/songwriter & business mogul

Luck is when an opportunity comes along and you're prepared for it.

—DENZEL WASHINGTON
  actor

It is your character, and your character alone, that will make your life happy or unhappy.

—JOHN MCCAIN
former US senator from Arizona &
US Navy captain

Find out who you are and do it on purpose.

—DOLLY PARTON
country music icon

Life is an improvisation. You have no idea what's going to happen next, and you are mostly just making things up as you go along.

—STEPHEN COLBERT
political commentator & television host

If your ship doesn't come in, swim out to it.

—JONATHAN WINTERS
actor & comedian

We can't take
any credit for
our talents.
It's how we
use them
that counts.

—MADELEINE L'ENGLE
fantasy author

Don't ever make decisions based on fear. Make decisions based on hope and possibility. Make decisions based on what should happen, not what shouldn't.

—MICHELLE OBAMA
author, attorney & former first lady of the United States

We must travel in the direction of our fear.

—JOHN BERRYMAN
  poet

It's really easy to fall into the trap of believing that what we *do* is more important than what we *are*. Of course, it's the opposite that's true: What we *are* ultimately determines what we *do*!

—FRED ROGERS
children's television host

Whenever you have to choose between being at peace or proving yourself right, choose the way of peace.

—JUAN MANUEL SANTOS
former president of Colombia & Nobel Prize winner

Be true to you and that should make the ride a little more interesting.

—WHOOPI GOLDBERG

comedian, television personality & actor

You should not underestimate the power you have to affirm the dignity and humanity of every human being.

—BRYAN STEVENSON

lawyer & founder of the Equal Justice Initiative

Contrary to what TV sells us, fame is not a profession. Be careful not to confuse fame and status and money with actual things that actually matter— like happiness and humanity and kindness.

—KAL PENN
actor & member of the Obama administration

Nice guys finish first—if you don't know that, then you don't know where the finish line is.

—GARRY SHANDLING
comedian, actor & writer

Don't wait for good things to happen to you. If you go out and make some good things happen, you will fill the world with hope. You will fill yourself with hope.

—BARACK OBAMA
44th president of the United States

You still have
a lot of time to
make yourself
be what you
want.

—S. E. HINTON
  author

Do not lose your sense of humor. You can have no idea at this point in your life how much you are going to need it to get through. . . . Humor is the most powerful, most survival-essential quality you will ever have or need to navigate through the human experience.

—JERRY SEINFELD
  comedian, sitcom star & philanthropist

One of the biggest mistakes you can make in life is to accept the known and resist the unknown. You should, in fact, do exactly the opposite: challenge the known and embrace the unknown.

—GUY KAWASAKI
venture capitalist

Minister to the world in a way that can change it. Minister radically in a real, active, practical, get-your-hands-dirty way.

—CHIMAMANDA NGOZI ADICHIE
author & speaker

The world is more malleable than you think, and it's waiting for you to hammer it into shape.

—BONO

rock star

We have, if we're lucky, about 30,000 days to play the game of life. And trust me, that's not morbid. In fact, it's wisdom that will put all the inevitable failures and rejections and disappointments and heartbreaks into perspective.

—ARIANNA HUFFINGTON
founder of HuffPost

Don't be afraid
to take risks,
because that's
where the
magic happens.

—MIRANDA JULY
filmmaker & author

You have brains in your head.
You have feet in your shoes.
You can steer yourself any
direction you choose.
You're on your own.
And you know what you know.
And YOU are the guy who'll
decide where to go.

—DR. SEUSS
children's author

TWO

Getting Started

Start where you are.
Use what you have.
Do what you can.

—ARTHUR ASHE
tennis great

Everybody always thinks you've got to go do something big and grand. I'll tell you where you start. You start by being good to at least one other person every single day. Just start there. That's how you begin to change the world.

—OPRAH WINFREY
television personality, philanthropist & CEO

Your inexperience is an asset, and will allow you to think in original and unconventional ways. Accept your lack of knowledge and use it as your asset.

—NATALIE PORTMAN
  actor

There's this dangerous, pervasive narrative around how your course of study in college needs to connect to the first steps you take after college. This narrative is a lie. I studied psychology in college and became a comedian—and you know what? It was the perfect education for me and my career path.

—ILANA GLAZER
comedian & writer

Do what you
have to do that
allows for the
most space
for what you
want to do.

—LIN-MANUEL MIRANDA
composer, lyricist & actor

I deeply understand what
it means to need to make a
living. . . . Take the job that
pays the bills if you need to.
Move to the city where
you can get employment.
Don't ignore or give up
your dreams though.
Claw your way back to them.

—YAMICHE LÉONE ALCINDOR
journalist & news correspondent

Your story does
not have to have a
traditional arc. There
is an Igbo saying which
translates literally
to, "Whenever you
wake up, that is your
morning." What matters
is that you wake up.
The world is calling you.

—CHIMAMANDA NGOZI ADICHIE
  author & speaker

Don't let your inability to do everything undermine your determination to do something.

—CORY BOOKER
  US senator from New Jersey

Great people do things before they're ready. They do things before they know they can do it. . . . Doing what you're afraid of, getting out of your comfort zone, taking risks like that—that's what life is.

—AMY POEHLER
comedian & writer

I hope you realize that every day is a fresh start for you. That every sunrise is a new chapter in your life waiting to be written.

—JUANSEN DIZON
author

Life is like trying to cross a big flowing river with lots of rocks and boulders strewn about. If you want to cross the river, you have to start on the bank and look at the first several rocks in front of you. You can wiggle them with your toe and sort of scan a few boulders out. But at some point, you've just got to pick one and jump, because the river is dynamic and always changing.

—MARK ROBER
content creator & inventor

THREE

Ambition & Action

There's nothing wrong with being driven. And there's nothing wrong with putting yourself first to reach your goals.

—SHONDA RHIMES
television producer, writer & CEO

Make an effort. Just pure, stupid, no-real-idea-what-I'm-doing-here effort. Effort always yields a positive value, even if the outcome of the effort is absolute failure of the desired result. This is a rule of life. "Just swing the bat and pray" is not a bad approach to a lot of things.

—JERRY SEINFELD
comedian, sitcom star & philanthropist

There is no stronger motivation than knowing that when you're not practicing, someone else is.

—MICHELLE KWAN

Olympic figure skater & US ambassador

You have to have insane confidence in yourself, even if it's not real. You need to be your own cheerleader now, because there isn't a room full of people waiting with pompoms saying, "You did it!" . . . I'm giving you permission to root for yourself. And while you're at it, root for others around you too.

—MINDY KALING
actor, writer & producer

Your life does not get better by chance. It gets better by change.

—JIM ROHN
author & motivational speaker

Do stuff you will enjoy thinking about and telling stories about for many years to come. Do stuff you will want to brag about.

—RACHEL MADDOW

television host & political commentator

It's not bragging if you can back it up.

—MUHAMMAD ALI
legendary boxer & activist

My favorite animal is the turtle. The reason is that in order for the turtle to move, it has to stick its neck out. There are going to be times in your life when you're going to have to stick your neck out. There will be challenges, and instead of hiding in a shell, you have to go out and meet them.

—DR. RUTH WESTHEIMER
sex therapist & talk show host

It's amazing
what you
can get if
you quietly,
clearly, and
authoritatively
demand it.

—MERYL STREEP
actor

At this moment in history,
leadership is calling us to say:
Give me the effing ball.
Give me the effing job.
Give me the same pay
the guy next to me gets.
Give me the promotion.
Give me the microphone.
Give me the Oval Office.
Give me the respect I've
earned, and give it to my
wolf pack too.

—ABBY WAMBACH
National Soccer Hall of Famer

Maybe the yes comes
before the readiness.
Maybe you say yes
and then you become
equipped to handle
whatever is about
to happen.

—GLENNON DOYLE
author, podcaster & activist

Internally, knowing your limits keeps you humble, motivated, and focused on a goal to point your finger toward. Externally, knowing the limits that are set for you by others gives you a place to point a different finger—I am talking about the middle one.

—MICHELLE YEOH
actor

Thinking will not overcome fear, but action will.

—W. CLEMENT STONE
businessperson & philanthropist

Don't follow your passion,
follow your talent. Determine
what you are good at (early), and
commit to becoming great at it.
You don't have to love it, just don't
hate it. If practice takes you from
good to great, the recognition and
compensation you will command
will make you start to love it. And,
ultimately, you will be able to shape
your career and your specialty to
focus on the aspects you enjoy
the most. And if not—make good
money and then go follow
your passion.

—SCOTT GALLOWAY
podcaster, author & speaker

In any given
moment we have
two options.
To step forward
into growth
or to step back
into safety.

—ABRAHAM MASLOW
psychologist & scholar

If you run into a wall, don't turn around and give up. Figure out how to climb it.

—MICHAEL JORDAN
basketball Hall of Famer & businessperson

Like I always say, you have to put some wings on them dreams, and some feet and fingers and some hands. They gotta get into some stuff. You can't just sit around and think of all the things you want to do. You've got to think of what you want to do, and then you've got to get out and make that happen.

—DOLLY PARTON
country music icon

You can't climb the ladder of success with your hands in your pockets.

—ARNOLD SCHWARZENEGGER

actor & former governor of California

Never be afraid to raise your voice for honesty and truth and compassion against injustice and lying and greed. If people all over the world ... would do this, it would change the earth.

—WILLIAM FAULKNER
Nobel Prize–winning author & screenwriter

Every story you've ever connected with, every leader you've ever admired, every puny little thing that you've ever accomplished is the result of taking action. You have a choice. You can either be a passive victim of circumstance or you can be the active hero of your own life.

—BRADLEY WHITFORD
actor & producer

It's okay to map out your future—but do it in pencil.

—JON BON JOVI
rock star

You can't wait for inspiration. You have to go after it with a club.

—JACK LONDON
author & journalist

If you feel like there's something out there that you're supposed to be doing, if you have a passion for it, then stop wishing and just do it.

—WANDA SYKES
comedian & actor

I am not lucky. You know what I am? I am smart, I am talented, I take advantage of the opportunities that come my way and I work really, really hard. Don't call me lucky. Call me a badass.

—SHONDA RHIMES
television producer, writer & CEO

If your uniform isn't dirty, you haven't been in the game.

—BEN BERNANKE

economist & former chair of the Federal Reserve

FOUR

Work Ethic

Whatever the problem, be part of the solution. Don't just sit around raising questions and pointing out obstacles.

—TINA FEY
comedian, writer & producer

No job or task is too small or beneath you. If you want to get ahead, volunteer to do the things no one else wants to do, and do it better.

—BOBBI BROWN
makeup artist & author

Work hard, be kind, and amazing things will happen.

—CONAN O'BRIEN

comedian, television personality & podcaster

A lot of people give up just before they're about to make it. You never know when that next obstacle is going to be the last one.

—CHUCK NORRIS
actor & martial artist

Do.
Or do not.
There is
no try.

—YODA

mentor & Jedi master

If opportunity doesn't knock, build a door.

—MILTON BERLE
comedian, radio star & actor

If you're offered a seat on a rocket ship, don't ask what seat! Just get on.

—SHERYL SANDBERG

tech executive, author & philanthropist

Opportunity is missed by most people because it is dressed in overalls and looks like work.

—THOMAS EDISON
inventor

There's a saying that if you do what you love, you'll never work a day in your life. At Apple, I learned that's a total crock. You'll work harder than you ever thought possible, but the tools will feel light in your hands.

—TIM COOK
CEO of Apple

It can take a long time to be as good as you want to be. Be kind to yourself during that period. And work hard.

—IRA GLASS
radio host

If you can't get in the front door, go through the back door.

—JAY LENO
comedian & talk show host

Hard work beats talent when talent doesn't work hard.

—TIM NOTKE
author & basketball coach

What looks like multitasking is really switching back and forth between multiple tasks, which reduces productivity and increases mistakes by up to 50 percent.

—SUSAN CAIN
author & lecturer

Be a doer, not a dreamer.

—SHONDA RHIMES

television producer, writer & CEO

Talent is cheaper than table salt. What separates the talented individual from the successful one is a lot of hard work.

—STEPHEN KING
legendary horror author

Effortless is a myth.

—ROGER FEDERER

tennis legend

Be a worker among workers. . . . It's more important that you fit in before you stick out.

—DAVID CARR
  writer & newspaper editor

I love it when people doubt me. It makes me work harder to prove them wrong.

—DEREK JETER
baseball Hall of Famer

Be the hardest
working person
you know.
Because if you're
not, someone
else will be.

—IAN BRENNAN
television writer & producer

Do the best that you can until you know better. Then when you know better, do better.

—MAYA ANGELOU
author, poet & activist

If I had nine hours to chop down a tree, I'd spend the first six sharpening my axe.

—ATTRIBUTED TO ABRAHAM LINCOLN
16th president of the United States

It takes as much energy to wish as it does to plan.

—ELEANOR ROOSEVELT

former first lady of the United States & activist

If you've done
your homework,
you developed the
ability to react to
the unknown,
then go out
and give the
unknown a try.

—GAYLE KING
television personality

There are no secrets for success. It is the result of preparation, hard work, and learning from failure.

—COLIN POWELL
former secretary of state & US Army general

I always tell my kids if you lay down, people will step over you. But if you keep scrambling . . . someone will always, always give you a hand. . . . But you've got to keep dancing. You've got to keep your feet moving.

—MORGAN FREEMAN
actor

FIVE

Success & Failure

When we show up, act boldly, and practice the best ways to be wrong, we fail forward.

—STACEY ABRAMS
politician & activist

My dad encouraged us to fail.
Growing up, he would ask us
what we failed at that week.
If we didn't have something,
he would be disappointed.
It changed my mindset at an
early age that failure is not the
outcome, failure is not trying.

—SARA BLAKELY
businessperson & philanthropist

I've missed over nine thousand shots in my career. I've lost almost three hundred games. Twenty-six times I've been trusted to take the game-winning shot and missed. I've failed over and over and over again in my life. And that is why I succeed.

—MICHAEL JORDAN
basketball Hall of Famer & businessperson

Don't put off till tomorrow what you can do today.

—BENJAMIN FRANKLIN

inventor & Founding Father

If we'd all stuck with our first dream, the world would be overrun with cowboys and princesses. So whatever your dream is right now, if you don't achieve it, you haven't failed, and you're not some loser.

—STEPHEN COLBERT
political commentator & television host

The best in the world are not the best because they win every point. It's because they know they'll lose again and again and have learned how to deal with it . . . Be relentless. Adapt and grow. Work harder. Work smarter.

—ROGER FEDERER
tennis legend

I don't like
to lose—at
anything. Yet
I've grown
most not from
victories, but
setbacks.

—SERENA WILLIAMS
tennis great & Olympic gold medalist

Never let a good crisis go to waste. It's the universe challenging you to learn something new and rise to the next level of your potential.

—TIM FERRISS
self-help author & podcaster

The thing about luck is that you have to be prepared to meet it. It's just one ingredient out of many. Sometimes you have to nudge fortune a little, sometimes badger fortune and keep trying. Because luck is never enough.

—CHIMAMANDA NGOZI ADICHIE
  author & speaker

Nobody is paying attention to your failure. The world is full of people failing. People are failing all around you. Failure is boring. . . . Only you will remember your failure. Unless you're the person that made the Samsung Galaxy S7. Those are the phones that literally explode. Everyone knows that person's failure.

—KUMAIL NANJIANI
comedian, actor & writer

Create your own definition of success. Don't let society tell you what it has to be.

—LENA WAITHE
writer, producer & actor

I learned many great lessons from my father, not the least of which was that you can fail at what you don't want, so you might as well take a chance on doing what you love.

—JIM CARREY
comedian & actor

If you really
look closely,
most overnight
successes took
a long time.

—STEVE JOBS
cofounder of Apple

For every winner, there doesn't have to be a loser. In fact, most success stories are less about competition and more about collaboration. The truth is, I could not have done any of this alone.

—MICHELLE YEOH
actor

The best things in my
life have often come
from things I viewed as
a disaster, as a mistake,
getting knocked down,
and getting broken,
being shattered.

—CORY BOOKER
US senator from New Jersey

It's easier to remember our failures and when we gave up, but you have to ask yourself: What were the moments where you kept fighting through the struggle and then you succeeded?

—DEMI LOVATO
pop star & actor

If I don't have
at least four or
five failures a
month, I feel like
I'm not trying
hard enough.

—RAMIT SETHI
author, entrepreneur & podcaster

Success is not final. Failure is not fatal. It's the courage to continue that counts.

—UNKNOWN

Eighty percent of success in your career will come from just showing up. The world is run by those who show up . . . not those who wait to be asked.

—STEVE BLANK
entrepreneur & author

Reggie Jackson struck out 2,600 times in his career, the most in the history of baseball, but you don't hear about the strikeouts. People remember the home runs. Fall forward. Thomas Edison conducted one thousand failed experiments. Did you know that? I didn't know that. Because the 1,001st was the light bulb.

—DENZEL WASHINGTON
actor

I have not failed. I've just found ten thousand ways that won't work.

—THOMAS EDISON
inventor

The unofficial motto in Silicon Valley is "Fail early and often." Almost no one gets it right the first, second, or even third time. Failure is baked into the innovation process; it's how they learn what doesn't work so they can home in on what does.

—RESHMA SAUJANI
lawyer, activist & founder of Girls Who Code

There are few things more liberating in this life than having your worst fear realized. . . . Today I tell you that whether you fear it or not, disappointment will come. The beauty is that through disappointment you can gain clarity, and with clarity comes conviction and true originality.

—CONAN O'BRIEN
comedian, television personality & podcaster

Don't be afraid of fear. Because it sharpens you, it challenges you, it makes you stronger, and when you run away from fear, you also run away from the opportunity to be your best possible self.

—ED HELMS
comedian & actor

You miss 100 percent of the shots you don't take.

—WAYNE GRETZKY
ice hockey legend

You will stumble and fall, you will experience both disaster and triumph, sometimes in the same day, but it's really important to remember that like a hangover, neither triumphs nor disasters last forever.

—HELEN MIRREN
  actor

Nobody else is paying as much attention to your failures as you are. . . . To everyone else, it's just a blip on the radar screen, so just move on.

—JERRY ZUCKER
producer, director & writer

Just as nature takes every obstacle, every impediment, and works around it—turns it to its purposes, incorporates it into itself—so, too, a rational being can turn each setback into raw material and use it to achieve its goal.

—MARCUS AURELIUS
Roman emperor & philosopher

For my first show at *SNL*, I wrote a Bill Clinton sketch, and during our read-through, it wasn't getting any laughs. This weight of embarrassment came over me, and I felt like I was sweating from my spine out. But I realized, "Okay, that happened, and I did not die." You've got to experience failure to understand that you can survive it.

—TINA FEY
  comedian, writer & producer

The truth is, whatever game you play in life, sometimes you're going to lose. . . . But negative energy is wasted energy. You want to become a master at overcoming hard moments. That is, to me, the sign of a champion.

—ROGER FEDERER
tennis legend

How we spend
our days is,
of course,
how we spend
our lives.

—ANNIE DILLARD
  author

A failure often does not have to be a failure at all. However, you have to be ready for it—will you admit when things go wrong? Will you take steps to set them right?—because the difference between triumph and defeat, you'll find, isn't about willingness to take risks. It's about mastery of rescue.

—ATUL GAWANDE
surgeon, author & public health researcher

Never let the
fear of striking
out keep you
from playing
the game.

—BABE RUTH
baseball legend

The only difference between a good shot and a bad shot is if it goes in or not.

—CHARLES BARKLEY

television personality & basketball Hall of Famer

You can measure your worth by your dedication to your path, not by your successes or failures.

—ELIZABETH GILBERT
author

SIX

Tuning In

Trust your gut, keep throwing darts at the dartboard. Don't listen to the critics—and you will figure it out.

—WILL FERRELL
actor, comedian & writer

For the most important decisions in your life: Trust your intuition and then work with everything you have to prove it right.

—TIM COOK
CEO of Apple

Asking smart questions, searching for the truth, learning to spot the red herrings are critically important. But I worry that listening gets short shrift. When I say listening, I'm speaking of more than just hearing the words, but hearing the meaning and the perspective and the experiences of others.

—LESTER HOLT
journalist & news anchor

Make a point of reaching out to people whose beliefs and values differ from your own. I would like you to listen to them, truly listen, and try to understand them, and find that common ground.

—JUSTIN TRUDEAU
23rd prime minister of Canada

Life is always talking to us. This is
what I do know. When you tap into
what it's trying to tell you, when
you can get yourself quiet enough
to listen—really listen—you can
begin to distill the still, small voice,
which is always representing the
truth of you, from the noise of the
world. You can start to recognize
when it comes your way.

—OPRAH WINFREY
television personality, philanthropist & CEO

When you really listen to
people, when you listen as
fiercely as you want to be
heard, when you respect the
idea that you are sharing the
earth with other humans,when
you lead with your nice foot
forward, you'll win every time.

—KRISTEN BELL
  actor

We have two ears and one mouth so that we can listen twice as much as we speak.

—ATTRIBUTED TO EPICTETUS
Greek philosopher

Be real. Be kind.
Take time to volunteer.
Pay your taxes.
Make your bed. . . .
And most of all, listen.
Listen to your hearts.
Listen to the hearts
of others.
Be the difference,
and be loud.

—MARLEE MATLIN
  actor

If you don't
like the road
you're walking,
start paving
another one!

—DOLLY PARTON
country music icon

When you have trouble making up your mind about something, tell yourself you'll settle it by flipping a coin. But don't go by how the coin flips; go by your emotional reaction to the coin flip. Are you happy or sad it came up heads or tails?

—DAVID BROOKS
political & cultural commentator

Everyone you will ever meet knows something that you don't. . . . Respect their knowledge. Learn from them.

—BILL NYE
science educator & television personality

That luminous part of you that exists beyond personality—your soul, if you will—is as bright and shining as any that has ever been. Bright as Shakespeare's, bright as Gandhi's, bright as Mother Teresa's. Clear away everything that keeps you separate from this secret luminous place. Believe it exists, come to know it better, nurture it, share its fruits tirelessly.

—GEORGE SAUNDERS
author

How do you know what is the right path to choose to get the result that you desire? The honest answer is this: You won't. And accepting that greatly eases the anxiety of your life experience.

—JON STEWART
comedian, writer & political commentator

Know that not everything requires an instant, immediate response. Take a chance. Learn to pause, to be silent, to pick your moment based on knowledge and full understanding.

—LESTER HOLT
journalist & news anchor

When you are listening to someone you respect, treat their whispers like screams.

—RAMIT SETHI
author, entrepreneur & podcaster

SEVEN

Mindset

The mind is like tofu.
It tastes like whatever you
marinate it in.

—SYLVIA BOORSTEIN
author, therapist & Buddhist teacher

Cynicism has never won a war or cured a disease or started a business or fed a young mind, or sent men into space. Cynicism is a choice. Hope is a better choice.

—BARACK OBAMA
44th president of the United States

Don't be reckless with what you've been given. Take what you do and how you live your life seriously.

—RAHM EMANUEL

US ambassador & former mayor of Chicago

I stand before you, a weird person. . . . Respect the need to be something very odd, not what is expected. Get to know yourself. Accept who you are, and love that person. . . . You already are everything you need to be.

—JENNIFER COOLIDGE
   actor

Each moment
is a procession
from the future
into the past, and
the sweet spot
is always the
present. Live in
that sweet spot.
Be present.

—WYNTON MARSALIS
musician, composer & artistic director of Jazz at Lincoln Center

Ralph Waldo Emerson once asked what we would do if the stars only came out once every thousand years. No one would sleep that night, of course. . . . We would be ecstatic, delirious, made rapturous by the glory of God. Instead the stars come out every night, and we watch television.

—PAUL HAWKEN
environmentalist, author & activist

You become what you think about all day long.

—ATTRIBUTED TO
RALPH WALDO EMERSON

essayist, philosopher & poet

Any time you say
something negative
about yourself,
also say something
positive. You can be
your biggest critic as
long as you're also your
biggest cheerleader.

—NOAH KAGAN
entrepreneur & tech innovator

It is not happiness
that makes us
grateful, it is
gratefulness that
makes us happy.

—DAVID STEINDL-RAST
monk, author & lecturer

When you're wide open, the world is a good place.

—SHARON SALZBERG

author & Buddhist teacher

We all go through life bristling at our external limitations, but the most difficult chains to break are inside us.

—BRADLEY WHITFORD
actor & producer

I believe, because I've done a little of this myself, pretending to be courageous is just as good as the real thing.

—DAVID LETTERMAN
talk show host

You are not supposed to be happy all the time. Life hurts and it's hard. Not because you're doing it wrong, but because it hurts for everybody. Don't avoid the pain. You need it. It's meant for you. Be still with it, let it come, let it go, let it leave you with the fuel you'll burn to get your work done on this earth.

—GLENNON DOYLE
author, podcaster & activist

When things are going sweetly and peacefully, please pause a moment, and then say out loud, "If this isn't nice, what is?"

—KURT VONNEGUT
author & satirist

Find something where you love the good parts and don't mind the bad parts too much. The torture you're comfortable with. This is the golden path to victory in life.

—JERRY SEINFELD
comedian, sitcom star & philanthropist

The corollary to carpe diem . . . is gratitude, gratitude for simply being alive, for having a day to seize. The taking of breath, the beating of the heart. Gratitude for the natural world around us—the massing clouds, the white ibis by the shore. In Barcelona, a poetry competition is held every year. There are three prizes: The third prize is a rose made of silver, the second prize is a golden rose, and the first prize: a rose. A real rose. The flower itself. Think of that the next time the term "priorities" comes up.

—BILLY COLLINS
former poet laureate of the United States

Be curious, not cool. Insecurity makes liars of us all.

—KEN BURNS
documentarian

Don't let anyone tell you that you can't do something, especially not yourself. Go conquer the world. Just remember this: Why not you? You made it this far.

—MINDY KALING
writer & producer

You are the one that possesses the keys to your being. You carry the passport to your own happiness.

—DIANE VON FURSTENBERG
fashion designer & businessperson

Just believe in yourself. Even if you don't, pretend that you do and, at some point, you will.

—VENUS WILLIAMS
tennis great & Olympic gold medalist

If you know you are on the right track, if you have this inner knowledge, then nobody can turn you off . . . no matter what they say.

—BARBARA MCCLINTOCK
scientist

You can't carry all things. . . . Decide what is yours to hold and let the rest go. Oftentimes, the good things in your life are lighter anyway, so there's more room for them.

—TAYLOR SWIFT
singer/songwriter & global icon

You can't wait
for inspiration.
You have to go
after it with
a club.

—JACK LONDON
novelist & journalist

You don't have to
have a dream. . . .
I advocate
passionate
dedication to
the pursuit of
short-term goals.

—TIM MINCHIN
comedian, actor & songwriter

To be fully alive, fully human, and completely awake is to be continually thrown out of the nest. To live fully is to be always in no-man's-land, to experience each moment as completely new and fresh.

—PEMA CHÖDRÖN
American Buddhist nun, author & teacher

There's great value in being able to step back and laugh at yourself, at life, and at attitudes.

—JIM HENSON
puppeteer, animator & filmmaker

Each of us has something which no one else has— or ever will have— something inside which is unique to all time.

—FRED ROGERS
children's television host

EIGHT

Self-Care

Do what you feel you want to do while also considering how you'll feel the next day.

—AMY SCHUMER
comedian, actor & producer

If you make your bed every morning you will have accomplished the first task of the day. It will give you a small sense of pride, and it will encourage you to do another task and another and another. By the end of the day, that one task completed will have turned into many tasks completed.

—WILLIAM H. MCRAVEN
US Navy four-star admiral

My message to you today is one that I learned the hard way: that there is nothing selfish about self-care, because if you don't take care of yourself, you won't change the world—but if you do, you just might.

—JASON KANDER
politician & author

Take care of your damn teeth.

—PATTI SMITH
rock legend & author

In our digital distraction we've lost a basic truth: fresh air, sunlight, and movement make us feel better.

—DR. JULIE HOLLAND
psychiatrist & author

Structure is something that calms our nature; we know this of toddlers.

—KRISTA TIPPETT
radio host & author

We need a lot more wonder and a lot more silence in our lives.

—FRED ROGERS

children's television host

You have to dance a little bit before you step out into the world because it changes the way you walk.

—SANDRA BULLOCK
  actor

You are not a slacker if you cut yourself some slack. . . . Take time to nurture your relationships, to celebrate your successes, and to recover from your losses.

—BILL GATES
cofounder of Microsoft

Spend your free time the
way you like, not the way you
think you're supposed to.
Stay home on New Year's Eve
if that's what makes you happy.
Skip the committee meeting.
Cross the street to avoid
making aimless chitchat with
random acquaintances.
Read. Cook. Run. Write a story.
Make a deal with yourself that
you'll attend a set number of
social events in exchange for not
feeling guilty when you beg off.

—SUSAN CAIN
author & lecturer

Rest is a weapon.
What was
once seen as a
weakness is
now a strength.

—BRETT BARTHOLOMEW
performance coach & author

Be in nature,
which is always
perfect and where
nothing is binary.

—KEN BURNS

documentarian

It is indeed a radical act of love just to sit down and be quiet for a time by yourself.

—JON KABAT-ZINN
mindfulness teacher & author

Everyone should have their mind blown at least once a day.

—NEIL DEGRASSE TYSON

astrophysicist & author

Rest and laughter are the most spiritual and subversive acts of all. Laugh, rest, slow down.

—ANNE LAMOTT
author, political activist & speaker

You can't exercise your way out of a bad diet.

—DR. MARK HYMAN
physician & author

Take a moment, find a place of stress, pain, or tension in your body now. Let a slow easy inhale find its way to that place—be there. Let a long easy exhale soften it. Stay. Repeat until you feel the kindness and care you're giving to yourself.

—MARGARET TOWNSEND
breathwork coach & author

The amount of sleep required by the average person is five minutes more.

—WILSON MIZNER

playwright & raconteur

You will never find time for anything. If you want time you must make it.

—CHARLES BUXTON

philanthropist, writer & member of Parliament

NINE

Life Skills

The people who embrace discomfort at an early age will be much better prepared than those who are protected from it.

—JUSTIN WELSH
business consultant

Call your mom and dad once in a while. A time will come when you will want your own grown-up, busy, hypersuccessful children to call you.

—BEN BERNANKE

economist & former chair of the Federal Reserve

If you keep good food in your fridge, you will eat good food.

—ERRICK MCADAMS
certified personal trainer

Most people are rude and nice manners are the secret keys to the universe.

—AMY POEHLER
comedian & writer

The more time you spend on your phone, the lonelier you are—this is what the data shows—because human beings evolved to have face-to-face contact. . . . Limit your time on it to the times when you can be fully on the phone and, otherwise, be fully with people.

—JONATHAN HAIDT
social psychologist & author

It is a common experience that a problem difficult at night is resolved in the morning after the committee of sleep has worked on it.

—JOHN STEINBECK
Nobel Prize-winning author

Most people
do best with
seven to nine
hours of sleep.
Yes, nine.

—DR. FRANK LIPMAN
physician & author

What I regret most in my
life are failures of kindness.
Those moments when another
human being was there, in
front of me, suffering, and
I responded . . . sensibly.
Reservedly. Mildly. . . . It's
a little facile, maybe, and
certainly hard to implement,
but I'd say, as a goal in life,
you could do worse than:
Try to be kinder.

—GEORGE SAUNDERS
 author

Manners are a sensitive awareness of the feelings of others. If you have that awareness, you have good manners, no matter what fork you use.

—EMILY POST
etiquette expert

Always admit when you're wrong. You'll save thousands in therapy. . . and a few friendships too.

—HARVEY FIERSTEIN
actor & playwright

Please never lose eye contact.
This may not be a lesson you
want to hear from a person
who creates media,
but we are spending more
time looking down at our
devices than we are looking
at each other's eyes.

—STEVEN SPIELBERG
  filmmaker

If you want a simple formula for having a good day, then get a workout done and do your most important task before lunch. Knock out those two things by noon and you really feel like you're ahead of the day.

—JAMES CLEAR
self-help author

If you care about being thought credible and intelligent, do not use complex language where simpler language will do.

—DANIEL KAHNEMAN
Nobel Prize–winning psychologist & author

Biographies give you a unique peek into the lives of great people. Instead of learning from your own mistakes, why not learn from those who have come before you?

—NOAH KAGAN
entrepreneur & tech innovator

Reading makes me feel I've accomplished something, learned something, become a better person. Reading makes me smarter. Reading gives me something to talk about later on. Reading is the unbelievably healthy way my attention deficit disorder medicates itself.

—NORA EPHRON
humorist & screenwriter

You gain strength, courage, and confidence by every experience in which you really stop to look fear in the face. You are able to say to yourself, "I lived through this horror. I can take the next thing that comes along." You must do the thing you think you cannot do.

—ELEANOR ROOSEVELT
former first lady of the United States & activist

As soon as you get out of bed in the morning, ask yourself, "What's one thing I can do today to bring me closer to my goal?" By committing to one small task at a time, you'll be building up your mental muscles while you make progress.

—JOANNA GROVER
psychologist & author

TEN

Resilience

*You are the sky. Everything else—
it's just the weather.*

—PEMA CHÖDRÖN
American Buddhist nun, author & teacher

After my first show [at *SNL*], one review referred to me as "the most annoying newcomer in the new cast." I promptly put it up on the wall in my office, reminding myself that to some people I will be annoying—some people will not think I'm funny, and that that's okay.

—WILL FERRELL
actor, comedian & writer

I found that my life got bigger when I stopped caring about what other people thought about me. You will find yours will too. Stay focused on what really matters.

—TIM COOK
CEO of Apple

Just get fueled
by rejection,
you know.
Don't let it
take you down.
Let it fuel you.

—AUBREY PLAZA
actor, producer & comedian

Learn from every mistake, because every experience, encounter—and particularly your mistakes—are there to teach you and force you into being more who you are. And then figure out what is the next right move. And the key to life is to develop an internal moral, emotional GPS that can tell you which way to go.

—OPRAH WINFREY
television personality, philanthropist & CEO

Once we give
up searching for
approval . . . we often
find it easier to simply
say what needs to be
said, and thus earn
respect and approval.

—GLORIA STEINEM
feminist activist, speaker & writer

There are some people who will get you and some people who won't ... and that's fine.

—RESHMA SAUJANI
lawyer, activist & founder of Girls Who Code

Try to avoid granting yourself the status of the victim. . . . The moment that you place blame somewhere, you undermine your resolve to change anything.

—JOSEPH BRODSKY
Nobel Prize–winning poet & essayist

I was blessed with a mother who was in a constant state of wonder. . . . And whenever I'd complain or be upset about something, she would say to me: "Darling, change the channel. You are in control of the clicker. Don't replay the bad, scary movie."

—ARIANNA HUFFINGTON
founder of HuffPost

It's not easy, but if you accept your misfortune and handle it right, your perceived failure can become a catalyst for profound reinvention.

—CONAN O'BRIEN

comedian, television personality & podcaster

You're unhappy and you feel like a failure. PERFECT! Use that sad/angry/disappointed energy. Channel it into what you know, deep down in your heart, you love.

—HEATHER HAVRILESKY
  writer & humorist

In the middle of winter I at last discovered that there was in me an invincible summer.

—ALBERT CAMUS

philosopher, author & political activist

Remember: Your voice has power, and you have to use your voice, even if it shakes.

—ALLYSON FELIX
track & field Olympian

ELEVEN

Community

Find a group of people who challenge and inspire you, spend a lot of time with them, and it will change your life.

—AMY POEHLER
comedian & writer

Choose people who lift you up. Find people who will make you better.

—MICHELLE OBAMA
author, attorney & former first lady of the United States

What should young people do with their lives today? Many things, obviously. But the most daring thing is to create stable communities in which the terrible disease of loneliness can be cured.

—KURT VONNEGUT
author & satirist

I think people
who have faults
are a lot more
interesting than
people who don't.

—SPIKE LEE
director, producer, screenwriter & actor

You never know which places and experiences are going to shift your perspective until after you've left them behind and had some time to look back.

—QUINTA BRUNSON
actor, comedian, writer & producer

Don't forget the simple pleasures of life. For me, it is still sharing a meal or a bottle of wine with friends, the enjoyment of being together with family and friends to share. This is true happiness.

—JACQUES PÉPIN
world-renowned chef

If your friends have healthy habits, you are more likely to as well. So get healthy friends.

—DR. MARK HYMAN
  physician & author

People are either radiators or they're drains, and you need to spend time around the radiators—the people who radiate goodness and light and positivity. Not the drains—the people who drag you down.

—REESE WITHERSPOON
actor & producer

Building your community is how you change the world.

—LEBRON JAMES
basketball great

If we learn to open our hearts, anyone, including the people who drive us crazy, can be our teacher.

—PEMA CHÖDRÖN
American Buddhist nun, author & teacher

Look to allies where you wouldn't expect to find them, don't be afraid to lean on people and ask for support when you need it, and don't forget that teamwork goes a very long way.

—SERENA WILLIAMS
tennis great & Olympic gold medalist

The most important trip you may take in life is meeting people halfway.

—HENRY BOYE
author

Respect people with less power than you. . . . I don't care if you're the most powerful cat in the room, I will judge you on how you treat the least powerful.

—TIM MINCHIN
comedian, actor & songwriter

No matter what happens in life, be good to people. Being good to people is a wonderful legacy to leave behind.

—TAYLOR SWIFT

singer/songwriter & global icon

Work hard, be kind, and amazing things will happen.

—CONAN O'BRIEN

comedian, television personality & podcaster

TWELVE

Purpose

If you want happiness for an hour, take a nap. If you want happiness for a lifetime, help somebody.

—LARRY LUCCHINO
(FROM A CHINESE PROVERB)
Major League Baseball executive

There are two most powerful days in your life. The day you are born, and the day you discover why.

—BONIFACE MWANGI

Kenyan photojournalist & activist

Action is the only remedy to indifference: the most insidious danger of all.

—ELIE WIESEL

Nobel Prize–winning author,
political activist & humanitarian

Stand for something or you will fall for anything. Today's mighty oak is yesterday's nut that held its ground.

—ROSA PARKS
civil rights icon

Everything bad comes from change, but so does everything good.

—ALANA NEWHOUSE

writer, editor & founder of Tablet *magazine*

I challenge you
to find that thing
in the world that
feels like such
a deep moral
contradiction
that you cannot
be silent.

—RAPHAEL WARNOCK
pastor & US senator from Georgia

If you're willing to be flexible, you will find your true passion.
So don't restrict your options, and limit your potential, with arbitrary self-imposed deadlines.

—VALERIE JARRETT
former senior adviser to President Obama

We often tell our students, "The future's in your hands." But I think the future is actually in your mouth. You have to articulate the world you want to live in first.

—OCEAN VUONG
poet, essayist & novelist

Act as if
what you
do makes a
difference.
It does.

—WILLIAM JAMES
philosopher & psychologist

Do the good that is in front of you, even if it seems awfully small.

—SHARON SALZBERG
author & Buddhist teacher

Do all the good you can, for all the people you can, in all the ways you can, as long as you can.

—HILLARY CLINTON
former first lady of the United States, senator & secretary of state

Nothing in life is more liberating than to fight for a cause larger than yourself, something that encompasses you but is not defined by your existence alone.

—JOHN MCCAIN

former US senator from Arizona & US Navy captain

I am no longer accepting the things I cannot change. I am changing the things I cannot accept.

—ANGELA DAVIS
feminist, political activist & author

Find those with similar purpose. Those who share your passion. Those who inspire you, who make you laugh out loud, who help you push past your fear, and challenge you to think, to dream, and to be brave and bold.

—NICOLE HOCKLEY
cofounder of Sandy Hook Promise

When I was about twenty-eight, after a decade as a professional comedian, I realized one night in LA that the purpose of my life had always been to free people from concern.

—JIM CARREY
  comedian & actor

Life's most persistent and urgent question is, "What are you doing for others?"

—DR. MARTIN LUTHER KING JR.
civil rights leader

There is nothing more beautiful than finding your course as you believe you bob aimlessly in the current. Wouldn't you know that your path was there all along, waiting for you to knock, waiting for you to become. This path does not belong to your parents, your teachers, your leaders, or your lovers. Your path is your character defining itself more and more every day, like a photograph coming into focus.

—JODIE FOSTER
actor & filmmaker

Take a stand for what's right. Raise a ruckus and make a change. You may not always be popular, but you'll be part of something larger and bigger and greater than yourself.

—SAMUEL L. JACKSON
  actor

As you go out into the world, don't waste time on problems that have been solved. . . . Look for the rough spots, the problems that seem too big, the complexities that other people are content to work around. It's in those places that you will find your purpose. It's there that you can make your greatest contribution.

—TIM COOK
  CEO of Apple

When I dare to be powerful, to use my strength in the service of my vision, then it becomes less and less important whether I am afraid.

—AUDRE LORDE
author, poet & civil rights activist

Only if we understand can we care. Only if we care will we help.

—DR. JANE GOODALL
zoologist & primatologist

For me, I am driven by two main philosophies, know more today about the world than I knew yesterday. And along the way, lessen the suffering of others. You'd be surprised how far that gets you.

—NEIL DEGRASSE TYSON
astrophysicist & author

Molly Reade writes about wellness, happiness, relationships, and many other subjects. She's a great believer in the power of words to elevate, evolve, and heal. She lives in New York's lower Hudson Valley.